Flounders for Tea

Recollections of a Galloway childhood 1934-1945

Marion Gunther

http://www.fast-print.net/bookshop

FLOUNDERS FOR TEA:
RECOLLECTIONS OF A GALLOWAY CHILDHOOD 1934-1945

A catalogue record for this book is available from the British Library

ISBN 978-178456-291-5

First published 2016 by
FASTPRINT PUBLISHING
Peterborough, England.

Foreword

Driving through the Galloway countryside today with its green fields enclosed by dry stone walls; through the small towns and villages and past the farms and country houses, there is a sense of continuity but much has changed over the years. Many village shops have disappeared. Landed estates are often smaller; the big houses have sometimes been reduced in size or divided up into flats. Farming practices have changed greatly and there are many fewer people working on the land.

Even before the First World War, some of the big houses were rented out to wealthy industrialists. The war brought further change to the countryside and after the Second World War there was no going back to the ordered world of big houses with large numbers of indoor and outdoor staff.

Marion Gunther provides us with a fascinating glimpse of life on a country estate in the years running up to and during the Second World War. She had come to Cardoness in 1934 when her father was appointed butler there. Marion left at the end of the war when she was just eleven and the big house could no longer afford the services of a butler. Her account is, therefore, that of a child growing up in the Galloway countryside, close to the sea and in easy reach of the hills and witnessing life on the estate through the experiences of childhood - a world of gardeners and gamekeepers, of walking to the local school with its severe discipline, a world of tea with fruit cake and tattie scones. Marion provides us with a unique insight into a rural way of life which has completely changed.

David Steel

Contents

Introduction.. 7

The Place: our life in the Old Lodge................ 10

My friend Laurie.. 18

Running wild 20

My father - a butler's life.............................. 28

My mother 35

The War 39

Skyreburn School....................................... 41

The People

The Gordon Family............................. 43

Angus Gillespie, the shepherd 44

Angus Farmer, dry stane dyker 47

Charlie Broadfoot, head gardener.......... 49

Jim Davidson, fisherman 51

Willie McMath, head groom 53

Bob McCormick, gamekeeper 54

Dr Craig 56

Gatehouse of Fleet 57

Epilogue 60

Acknowledgements

I would like to thank my editor Annie Winner, who with dedication, time and patience has given me the confidence to put together these recollections. Without her help this book would not have been possible.

To my daughter Karen Croft and son Mark Gunther for their encouragement throughout the project. To my grand daugher Rebecca Croft for her practical advice, enthusiasm and emotional support.

Particiular thanks to David Steel for his invaluable input and to Sheila Wallace for her interest.

Galloway Hills

Rolling hills, gently sloping
Curving softly and serenely
Scottish hills In the lowlands
Ablaze with heather, draped as purple curtain
Over the sullen crags in the evening light.
Hiding amidst deep dark lochs,
Mysterious, and fringed by trees of fir and yew
Trout in abundance
Lie quietly in the waters
Curlews cry over the wilderness of moor.
The wild cat snarls and leaps after his prey
An adder, vicious tongued, coiled in the sun
Danger hidden, unsuspecting, in these hills of
beauty in the Lowlan

Introduction

Recalling an upbringing and way of life long vanished, I hope the following pages will evoke memories for some, and give pleasure to many. Names and places have not been changed and I apologise if there are any small inaccuracies. Many of the photographs were taken by my mother with her little box camera.

My mother with me aged 6 months

In August 1934, when I was six months old, my mother and father left Bromsgrove where I was born and went to live in Galloway on the Cardoness estate near Gatehouse-of-Fleet.

My mother with me outside Cardoness House

Until the war broke out in 1939 my father was head butler to Colonel and Mrs Rainsford-Hannay. My father was ideally suited for this job as he had been trained and climbed the ranks at St James's Palace.

My father in the grounds of St James's Palace

The salary for the position at Cardoness House was £80 a year. The Lodge was rent free and other perks were included such as a ton of coal per annum, and wood from the estate, fresh fish from the Solway, game and an abundance of vegetables. My mother, a Yorkshire lass, adapted well to life in the wilds.

Cardoness House

Photo courtesy Brian McMurray

Our predecessors at the Old Lodge, the Thom family

Photo courtesy Brian McMurray

For the next eleven years my childhood was idyllic and I could roam free through woods, over moors and along shores. This part of Galloway had a gentle beauty and the road from Gatehouse to Creetown is arguably one of the most beautiful stretches of coastline in the British Isles. My life over those eleven years is described in the following pages.

The Place: Our Life in the Old Lodge

The gated Lodge was one of two on the estate which led to the big house. It was very pretty. Beautiful shells from the shore lined the path – loads and loads of them - and surrounded the cottage, and the little garden was filled with sweet william and London pride in the borders. In the kitchen there was a black leaded grate and stove where all the home cooking was done – griddle scones, tattie scones, drop scones were made there. My mother could skin a rabbit and gut it, and pluck a pheasant.

A large scrubbed table with an oilcloth stood in the centre of the room where my mother sat sewing until late into the night, lit by a wonderful brass oil lamp She made all our clothes and helped with tailoring for the kilt maker, Mr McDavid, in Creetown. This was to earn some extra money. Once a red squirrel became tame and sat on the edge of the stove. This unnerved my mother at times, and eventually the gamekeeper caught it in a cloth and took it away up into the woods.

The Old Lodge, our home

Weekly baths in the tin hip bath by the fire were much looked forward to. The washhouse was fuelled by endless wood from the estate, some of which we gathered ourselves. It was filled with dense steam and my mother's clothes were pegged out spotless and starched on the clothes line in the wood. The clothes pegs were made by the local tinker people who came round and sold them.

Hair washing was a weekly ritual for me and my little sister. Rainwater was used, and after heating gently on the range, was then poured over our heads with the big white enamel jug. The soft water was good for our hair. Ann had ringlet rags threaded through her long hair, and mine stayed in natural tight curls and was vigorously brushed by mother.

A small scullery adjoined the main room where everything was kept on the stone flagged floor to keep cool. Tiny oil lamps lit the bedroom and the main room, which was approached by a narrow dark passage. My sister and I hid from the old tramp who banged with his stick on the door to have his tin can filled with hot tea. He had many layers of old coats tied around his middle with string. He was smelly and cross, and while I was undoubtedly afraid of him, he was in fact quite harmless.

Sometimes, to be out of my mother's way, I would sit under the deal table with a pack of playing cards, or quietly read as soon as I was able to. I loved picking and bunching snow drops to sell for one penny a bunch in Gatehouse, our nearest town. The bunches were neatly tied with cotton and accompanied by ivy leaves. This was a small source of income for my mother. My life revolved around my mother as my father was working long irregular hours as butler.

One job my mother set us when my sister was old enough to join me was gathering kindling sticks, dry bundles of beech twigs to light her fires. We went through the fence, across the fields and into the beech trees by the shore, staggering back with arms full of fuel. Across the field from our lodge and the beech wood, where Ann and I gathered these kindling sticks, there was a sloping, sandy bank on to the shore.

Surrounding the house were grassy hummocky dunes, where numerous rabbits lived. There were so many of them – larger than the usual wild species. Black in colour, or black and white, these were lovely creatures and multiplied greatly and became quite tame. Once, on sliding down, I disturbed the soft sand to reveal a huddle of newly born rabbits curled up in a hole. I was surprised at their nakedness, and how vulnerable they were to predators. I felt sad, and hoped the mother rabbit would find them

My mother with me holding my sister's teddy bear

There was just the one main room. I was a strange little girl really because I loved reading, and I sat under the table because it was peaceful and away from the clatter of cooking and things my mother was doing. There was a little radio and sometimes I would start to cry – why I do not know – and I asked for it to be turned off because I didn't really like it, and I wanted the peace and quiet of being under the table.

In our Christmas stocking there was always a book, some paper and crayons and things that my father had made, because, don't forget, there was very little, especially when the war came. There was nothing much at all. I loved the main room with the big black leaded range which my mother had to black lead all the time, and the trivet, where the big kettle hung over the fire and you could have other pots hanging from there as well. She was a very good cook (jam roly poly pudding steamed in cloths with homemade jam was a favourite) and the range was heated by the coal and wood which we were supplied with. We grew some potatoes but everything was provided.

We had wonderful food, all from the estate. The fishermen brought fish for my mother, dabs and flounders – the flounders were still flapping away when they were brought. The hens were local, and we walked to the dairy and had the milk straight from the cow, poured into a big jug - there was no pasteurisation or anything like that then - and pheasants at shooting time of course, and rabbits. So really we lived off the land and the vegetables were from the large garden on the estate – the estate was huge. There were lots of different tied cottages.

From the Old Lodge the drive up to Cardoness House was delightful. It was lined with multi coloured rhododendron bushes which backed on to a dense beech wood, and of course there were wonderful hiding places for hide and seek and so on. I had a special tree which was a very strange shape. I can see it now and on each side of it – I named each part of it – one branch was called Haggie and the other was called Keeka. Don't ask me why! I used to talk to these mythical creatures in this tree. When I was about 4 or 5 I loved climbing trees and once I literally got stuck in the fork of a tree. My friend Laurie was with me and it took some of the men from the estate to get up there and get me down. I got up beautifully and I really wasn't too bothered about coming down.

Me with my father and the rhododendrons

The bushes, which grew well owing to the mild gulf stream climate, were ideal for our games of hide and seek. Bluebells grew in profusion on the verge sides mingled with stitchwort followed by red campion, wild garlic and ragged robin. I remember picking large bunches of bluebells for Mother. These were put in a jam jar and only lasted a short time before flopping over. Bracken grew well with fronds as high as my head. This was wonderful for camp making when the fronds died.

Mother was always busy, it was quite hard work. One day she wondered where I was – I was about 3 or 4. There was a horse trough in the field where we climbed over to get sticks, and the trough was covered in leaves. I had a stick and I was a curious child so I was leaning over the trough and pressing with the stick and I fell in head first. My mother must have had a sort of premonition and out she came, and I was in the trough upside down. She pulled me out and held me by my ankles and just got the water out.

Before school I wasn't interested in dolls, but I did have one doll – a china doll – and I wanted just to walk up beyond the Lodge to the railings where there was this big horse. I wanted to show the horse my doll, and I had very, very golden coloured hair, covered in curls, sort of straw coloured. So I put my head through the railings and the horse came right up and I was talking to the horse and wanting to show it my doll. All I can remember is the horse's enormous home big brown teeth – it thought my hair was straw, clearly. I pulled my head away from the railings and ran back, crying, not bothered by the doll being damaged. Ever since then I've been very wary of horses.

Me at Kirkdale Bridge about 1937

There was a little bus which, en route to Carsluith, dropped off post and parcels to outlying houses. A friend of my mother's worked at Kirkdale House, and we used to visit her. The bus stopped at Kirkdale Bridge where a burn ran through a densely wooded area. I was about 4 years old and remember seeing a wild cat crouching near the bridge. The animal, much larger than a domestic cat, with a striking black and grey coat, stands out in my memory.

The winters in Galloway were usually mild, but my father had made sledges for us, and when snow did fall we walked to the slopes near Old Land, or Newton Farm to join the Baird boys for many hours of fun. I well remember tingling fingers and toes resulting in chilblains. An effective treatment for these was snowfire, a cool green ointment which Mother kept in readiness.

The gamekeeper's retirement cottage at Mossyard was a favourite place to visit, and I can well remember tea on the Sabbath, most definitely a day of rest. We would go on a local bus which was a great delight to me. We watched the rabbits from the window, and with luck, a deer grazing at the foot of the big fir wood. The bus grated and rattled upwards so the ribbon of the blue sea was soon visible from the window, territory which I had never visited. The pink washed cottage was in sight and the white gate open. We were welcomed by Mrs McCormick (the gamekeeper's wife) clad in a motherly apron. She and my mother would then settle by the window and I would be taken to the beehives at the end of the garden behind the privy. The heavy drone of bees and the strange sweet smell of honeycomb and the twang of the salt breeze from the shore was a constant delight to me. Bob McCormick told me how the bees worked and we looked very closely at the hives, and the golden liqueur was always presented to my mother.

The sumptuous tea laid out for us in the front parlour, surrounded by numerous ornaments, bric-a-brac, peacock feathers, family photos, was a somewhat gloomy affair, but it made up for the endless talking from my mother and Mrs McCormick. The food laid out on the lace tablecloth was delicious. Rich homemade fruit cake, followed by griddle scones, washed down with sweet goat's milk for me, and strong tea for the grownups. Then there were drop scones, tattie scones, fruit cake and gingerbread, all home made. On our very best behaviour, my sister and I sat on high straight backed chairs, while the light filtered through the tiny lattice windows. I found Mrs McCormick rather awesome. She was a member of the Plymouth Brethren. I cannot remember my father being there. Most surely he was busy at Cardoness House or away in the war.

We walked home before the sun set over the hill, past the black deep pond, past the farm gate, the next day's milk cans already out, bade good night to the pots and pans man with his horse and cart and were soon to reach the Old Lodge and for me the safety and cosiness of mother's dying embers in the black range.

The other gamekeeper's cottage lay near a pond which often froze over during the hard months and we would slide on the icy surface, making the edges crack. This was daring and exciting and, no doubt, dangerous. It was black and mysterious and my shoes wore out completely. This pond when really safe was used for skating by the Rainsford-Hannays.

Johnnie Baird lived in Newton farmhouse with his wife and large family. Mrs Baird was a plump jolly lady, and the large stone flagged kitchen area was alive with her happy six children. I remember the youngest shuffling bare-bottomed across the floor. I loved visiting, as a warm welcome awaited, with fresh mugs of milk and homemade fruit cake. The farm was mainly dairy, with large herds of cattle to supply the estate with milk, and also the Stewartry Dairy in Gatehouse.

The nearest village school was Skyreburn was about a mile away, and Gatehouse was about 2 ½ miles away. We had trips there on the bus, which was a two hourly one.

My Friend Laurie

My friend and daily companion, Laurie, lived in the big lodge a short distance away along a path between the beech trees and large ferns. I would walk through the wood at a very early age, before school, probably 3-4, to the big lodge and we were very good friends until he left. His father was a joiner and eventually they went to live in Canada. We were able to wander quite freely. That was absolutely wonderful – there was no fear because immediately outside you stepped into the lovely beech woods.

Me with Laurie on the rocks 1937

From an early age there was nothing to be afraid of, the population was so sparse, it was just the estate people. Laurie and I were inseparable, and during the long summer holidays we roamed the estate to find adventure. In great contrast to the Glasgow evacuees who were our school mates during the war, sometimes our playmates were children of the local rich families who were home from boarding school. Sometimes we were friends, and, on occasion, enemies, with stick fights in the woods. Protected by sitting in high forked beech trees, we threw sticks at our opponents who were below us. They thought it an advantage to be on the ground in order to make a quick getaway when the excitement became too scary.

Sometimes Laurie and I would wander beyond the beech woods near our homes to the woodland path leading to Old Land and Mill Knock where we found a deep, dark pond with a footbridge across the middle. This was out of bounds, but with little sense of time, and without fear, we sat there on the plank in the middle of the pond watching the wildlife around us, and the shadows in the water. My mother, although not unduly worried, alerted the estate workers, and a rescue party was sent out at dusk to search for us. After a good talking to, we decided not to venture there again.

Laurie and I spent many hours making and sitting in wigwam shaped tents enforced by a frame of strong sticks, then covered thickly in the brown fronds. This took place in the beech wood between the two lodges.

There was a big wall by the gate and we could run along that wall. That was great fun. It was quite a drop down on to the road, but there was hardly any traffic of course, just the old tramp and the occasional tradesman. Below the wall there was a wonderful area for playing peevie (hopscotch) just outside the lodge gate.

Running Wild

When old enough, from 6 onwards, I roamed the estate freely and without fear, completely together with Nature in all her glory. We made camps from dried fern fronds, whittled whistles from hazel and the ends of spent cartridges hammered together, and fashioned catapults with a hazel fork and knicker elastic. Fishing nets for shrimping in rock pools were made from old stockingette tied to a long stick. We went bird nesting and egg collecting on Seagull Island where the nests were abundant and occasionally we collected gulls' eggs which was not in fact illegal in those days. They were very tasty, rich and slightly salty.

My favourite place was the wild strawberry bed, where adders slithered to be whacked by Laurie with a withy stick. Often we saw two or three, if the peacocks kept at the big house in the grounds had not caught and killed them first. The strawberries, ripe and sharp on our tongues, were then worth the unknown danger of the adders. Handfuls gathered, we put them in grubby hankies and lay on the bare grey flat rocks and watched the sea birds wheeling overhead. Peewits or lapwings were a common sight and the mournful cry of the curlew echoed across the hills.

Mill Knock and Ben Jock were two distant gentle hills, where many picnics and much exploring took place. My mother always knew when it would rain as Mill Knock looked closer and almost threatening. There was a lovely walk, either by track or through old land, all through the woods to the hills. Curlews called and nested in these hills, where the purple heather covered the summits, and white heather was much sought after. Below the hill, bullocks grazed and streams trickled to bog land. I jumped from tussock to tussock and often sank alarmingly into the innocent looking green clumps. The climb was a gentle one, and at the cairn – the very summit stone – we rested and looked across at the magnificent Solway Bay. We followed the narrow rabbit tracks between the heather, sharp and springy, and ever watching for adders.

A black and white herd, Galloway breed of cattle, snorted and charged across a field. I ran, and escaped under a barbed wire fence. No doubt they meant no harm but were agitated by the numerous flies buzzing around their faces. My respect for large animals, especially cattle and horses, remains today.

And so my childhood passed. I remember endless sun drenched days of freedom. Barefooted and nimble, Laurie would chase me across the Solway sands until I fell exhausted and happy on the warm pebbles on the burn's edge at low tide. The bull rushes, a large green bed of sighing fronds shimmering in the summer breeze, hid us from the road and the crooked stones of Skybrigg. We would race over the mudflats as a challenge. The mudflats were forbidden and our mothers warned us never to cross them. One day I followed Laurie carefully, lightly, easing my gum boots out of the black oozing mud. Inch by inch, hand in hand, we squelched our way far out – it seemed then – mud covering our ankles, then to the tops of our little boots. Then – stuck! My foot left my boot in a neat dark hole. The challenge was over. We retreated and would always have a good skelping from our mothers over our muddy feet. It was always worth it, though.

Often we would cross the sand at low tide and race against time before the Fleet rose quickly with the incoming Solway tide. The firm sand beyond the nets was golden and rippled where the sand hoppers made little mounds, a great feeding place for oyster catchers and sand pipers. Sharp eyes found the nests of sand pipers, a shallow scooped out hole, beyond the tide mark on the soft pale sand. After high tide, rock pools would fill will multi-coloured crabs, bright greens and reds. Small fish and sticklebacks were caught in our home made nets, a piece of muslin or rayon stockingette tied to end of a piece of supple reed. Bright red anenomes curled inwards when touched and wet seaweed popped up as we slithered across the wet rocks between the clear pools. Climbing along the higher rocks at full tide was a challenge. Nimble bare feet were very sure. Clumps of sea pinks, or thrift, sheltered in sandy crevices and adders basked on the rocks before being frightened by our stick throwing.

Me and my sister Ann on Cardoness Shore 1943

During the last week of the long summer holidays we were expected to play nearer at hand. Our mothers liked to prepare for school and were busy lengthening and mending our clothes ready for the cooler weather. Taking my shrimp net, a supple peeled stick with an old foot of mother's lisle stocking tied securely on the end, I carefully and quietly passed Haggie and Keeka who were ignoring me and quarrelling fiercely and stamping their strange, twisted claw like roots on the earth. I wended my way, following the winding moss covered path, to the point, scrambling nimbly down the hard rocky edge to the shadowy pools below. The early morning sun slanted across the already incoming tide which would by midday cover the rock pools. It cast a curious light on the limpets and scarlet anenomes clinging to the damp rock surface.

I watched the shadows and called to the tern in fluttering isolation on the netting pole. Bending low, and dipping my net far down into the pool, I disturbed a small grey fish from the muddy bottom. Expertly twisting my net I caught two pale shrimps and put them safely in a shallow sandy pool. Later I would add other curious sea creatures. The scraping of the crab claws echoed in the rock fissures deep down. There were small almost transparent pink crabs, usually unobtainable; delicate green and red crabs with black inky markings; and larger dark green and brown ones with thick claws, in those dark fissures. I kept very still and watched an oyster catcher scavenging on the flotsam washed up by yesterday's tide. Lovely pink shells, as small as a finger nail, misty coloured winkles and razor shells were abundant, to be washed away on the new tide and replaced by others even more lovely.

Another adventure I remember was when the tide was way far out, as far as the end of the world, I thought. I walked with my friends Sam and Margaret and Ethel away past the long nets, curling up our toes on the rippled firm sand, and stopping to poke my fingers in the odd little whorls of sand thrown up by small sea creatures. Well past a long net, we could see the distant silver ribbon of the river Fleet which had to be crossed to reach the sandy shores beyond. Our keen knowledge of the tides and the exact timing allowed us to wade the river at its lowest and return knee deep as the tide came in. This indeed was an adventure and out of bounds, especially as Ethel was so slow and had to be pulled to make her hurry quickly. "Hurry Ethel or we will nae make it to the shallows" Sam called from a distance. With our dresses pulled up over our heads and the river heaving and swelling alarmingly, we pushed our small bodies against the current. Never before had the firmed ridged bank seemed so comforting as we pulled our tired bodies on to the ridge and silently headed for the long net.

The day was passing and the shadows were dark on the flat rocks, with yesterday's heavy seaweed tresses wet from the tide. We reached the footpath to the Big Lodge and home.

Me on my father's motorbike

My father had a motorbike and sidecar. I went in the sidecar because my sister was three years and eight months younger than myself so she wasn't much fun – she was too small . I remember once this wonderful trip when my father took me – he had time off occasionally – in the sidecar and we went to Glasgow. We went on the big Ferris wheel and it stopped when we were right at the very top. I can see that now – I wasn't a bit scared – I didn't know about fear then.

One or two trips like that stand out in my mind because they were few and far between.

My father with me and my sister Ann

There were two lodges and a beautiful fisherman's cottage just beyond the lodges, then further up, a lovely drive into the yard where the chauffeur lived in his tied cottage. Just beyond that there was this wonderful walled garden – there were quite a few gardeners – the head gardener was Mr Broadfoot. Once I legged it up the wall and there were delicious apricots and peaches growing against it - the climate was very mild because of the Gulf Stream - and the boys helped me to get up the wall to get the fruit. We pinched the neeps they had on Burns night.

My father, right, in the Home Guard before he was called up

I think my father was quite happy at Cardoness House but we didn't have an awful lot to do with the Rainsford-Hannays. They were old school – he was a colonel in the army.

They gave an annual party for the children on the estate and strangely enough that didn't impress me terribly. One year when my sister was about 18 months old we were at the Christmas party there, and all I can remember was her shuffling on her bottom across this carpet.

Some of the staff who worked in Cardoness House had a lovely tied cottage. My auntie Brenda worked there for a while – I don't think my father treated her very well.

My Father - A Butler's Life

My father was an only child, born in 1902 in Liverpool, and when he was a small boy his father decided to up and leave and go to Australia to make his fortune, leaving my father Harold with his mother Marion who had to work to keep them both.

My father (top left) and his mother (bottom right)

I think my grandfather came back as a very old man, and apparently he had made his fortune and other people reaped the rewards. My father was quite a lad about town before he married my mother, lots of girlfriends, all those flapper girls!

My father's father, Charles Bishop

After he finished his training at St James's Palace, my father's first job was at Belbroughton House. In due course, following an interview with Colonel Rainsford-Hannay, my father accepted the position of butler at Cardoness House in 1934. As the butler, my father was in charge of the staff that did the serving. There were three in the kitchen, Mrs Docherty as head cook, three in the pantry, three in the house, with two or three coming in to work as domestics; all my father's responsibility. The butler showed the two footmen how to clean silver, and place it on green baize in special drawers and cupboards. He was fully responsible for the wine cellar, and knew which wine to serve at table. Full evening dress was worn and a grey suit in the morning at breakfast. My father provided his own clothes, and they were laundered by my mother.

Dinner often involved duties until midnight when big parties were held. Glass and silver had to be put away afterwards.

At midday, he picked up the papers from the Lodge, and then enjoyed a short lunch break downstairs with the staff, and a cup of tea and a cake before the laying of the table for the evening meal at 8 pm. Tips from the guests were generous, which supplemented his salary. My father bought a small car – an Austin Seven, with this money. There was a little more time when the Rainsford-Hannays were away, and he was able to enjoy being with his wife and young daughters.

At these times we saw more of my father, and always looked forward to special family outings in his car. A memorable one was stopping at Ravens Hall on the way to Stranraer. Before arriving at Creetown the coast was rugged, with formidable jagged rocks and dark caves where sea rushed into little caves and pounded the rocks. Ravens nested here and as a 5 year old I found these large black birds, with their strange cries, exciting and somewhat awesome. Arriving at Stranraer in time for our picnic lunch, prepared by my mother, we sat on the grassy cliffs above the town and gazed across the sea. My father, with his binoculars, was fascinated by the ships crossing over to Ireland.

My mother in my father's first car

He was a very fit and athletic man, a great sportsman.

Centre forward, Sand Hutton hockey team

Ready for play

Mixed doubles Early 1930s

My father on one of his first motorbikes (late 1920s)

A picnic at Laundry Bay May 30 1943, taken to send to my father, me on the right

Letter from my father – he was already in the desert.

My dear Marion and Ann. I have just received two of Mummy's airmail letters that I had begun to think had gone astray. One of them November and one of December, telling me about Christmas which I so much wanted to know about. As I have just sent Mummy a letter I thought it would be nice to write to you so you can thank Mummy for them for me. I was glad to hear you had such a nice time at Christmas and I think you were very lucky to go to a big party again. I did not think there would be one with almost everything being rationed and so expensive, and then to another one at school. My word, you were both very lucky.

The book you had given to you certainly does sound very interesting. You look like being an expert in botany before very long. I expect you have really been a little disappointed not having any snow for that means you would not have any snowmen to make and no tobogganing, but Mummy tells me you have been sliding on the ice, so maybe you enjoyed that just as well.

Now I am wondering just how a bottle bomb managed to get on the shore. Maybe some military schemes had taken place there and it had got overlooked. Anyway I am glad no one was near it at the time it exploded and got hurt.

I hope Mummy fulfilled her promise and took you to the pictures and I expect that by the time you get this it will have been such a long time ago you will have forgotten. I haven't been to the pictures for a long time. I went to a funny little cinema when we first reached the desert. I don't suppose you ever thought there were such things as a cinema in the desert and talkie ones at that. When we were in Tripoli I did not see a picture show but I did see two very good concerts. One was given by the Highland Division's own concert party and the other was given by the Kiwis, the New Zealand soldiers. This was a very nice big band.

I was glad to hear you are being so helpful with the wood but I do hope you are very careful with that big axe. I really don't like the thought of you using it. You must be very careful if you do. How is the old garden? I remember you used to be a great help with the tatties and I hope you help to keep the weeds down like you used to. Ann, I am sure, will give you a hand now. That will be the day, when Daddy is back, throwing the tatties over to you again, and a game of rummy before you go to bed. Let's hope the time is not so far away. I am longing to see you all again and glad to hear you are doing so well at school, so keep it up and try and beat all the others. No doubt by the time you receive this Ann will have started too. Well I hope she doesn't get the strap as much as you did when you first started.

Well my dear, I must close once more. I hope you get my letter card in time for your birthday and that you had a very happy day and many more to come. With lots of love and big kisses to you and Ann. Ever your loving Daddy.

My father was with the Eighth Army, a driver, a Desert Rat, with Montgomery on the front line, El Alamein to Tripoli. He was away for four years. I think probably I missed him quite a lot. I've got lovely photographs of him before the war – there's a lovely one of me when I was small, about 2 or 3, on the rocks, he was sitting on a rock here, and I was sitting on his knee. He made me a beautiful dolls' house.

Me with my father on the rocks at Laundry Bay about 1936

Me with the dolls' house my father made for me

Anworth was situated within walking distance of Cardoness. You could follow a quiet lane off the main road from Gatehouse until you came to the little hamlet of Anworth. There were two churches – the old one in ruins, roofless and covered in ivy, and the new one nearby, surrounded by neat lawns, the manse and a few cottages by the burn. I remember our annual visit to the church service. We sat, in our Sunday best, with other estate workers and their families on hard seats towards the back of the church. The special enclosed pews were reserved for the Rainsford-Hannays. My father's ashes are buried in the well kept graveyard, and my mother's name, as she wished, has been added to the memorial stone.

The ruined church at Anworth

My Mother

My mother was born in 1911. She was a gamekeeper's daughter, and spent her childhood years with her two sisters and brother moving around to various estate lodges with her parents Herbert and Margaret Roper.

High Hoyland Lodge

My mother, the second eldest and the tomboy of the family, spent many hours with her father on the estate and learned to pluck pheasants, handle ferrets and skin rabbits.

She was a bright child and passed the entrance exam for grammar school but her destiny was to go into service in the big house in Sand Hutton where she met my father. They celebrated their engagement at Lulworth Cove.

My mother's youngest sister Brenda with ferrets

My grandfather Herbert Roper

My grandparents Herbert Margaret Roper

My parents' wedding 1932

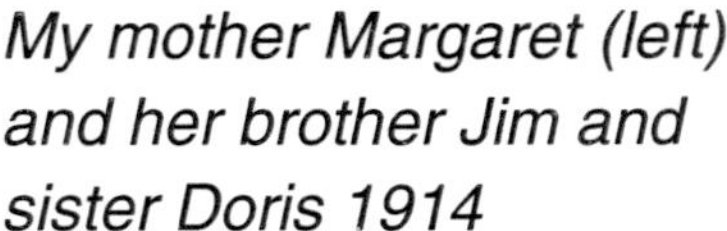

My mother Margaret (left) and her brother Jim and sister Doris 1914

When off duty, my parents enjoyed travelling by motor bike to visit dear friends Harold and Hilda King in Birmingham and to the TT races on the Isle of Man.

During the war I clearly remember a telegram arriving to say that my uncle Jim had been blown up in a minesweeper., I was 8 years old. My mother, no doubt grief stricken, acted calmly and quietly, not wanting to upset her small daughters.

Fond memories which stand out for me were my mother's picnics on the shores of Laundry Bay during the long summer months. Her basket, covered with a white cloth, was filled with homemade fruitcake and scones. Our table was a flat rock and while mother sewed, we played by damming a stream and making a fort, or climbing the battleship rock watching out for the enemy.

Picnic on Cardoness Shore 1941 me (far left) and Ann (third right) with "posh boys" David and Michael Short

The month of July was notorious for horse flies, locally known as clegs, which had nasty stings. The cure for any bite or sting was a dock leaf or, when at home, a bicarb soda mix. A favourite spot was a peaceful little cove on Cardoness shore when mother would take a pile of darning and keep an eye while we paddled in the oncoming tide.

I remember my mother saying to both of us as we were growing up a little bit "Do respect everyone, but I don't want you to madam this and madam that." I remember that clearly, because I suspect she thought with her girls growing up that she probably didn't want them to go into service.

To sum up, my mother was hardworking, capable and most of all a caring and loving person. She always said that those 11 years at Cardoness were the happiest of her life.

The War

We stayed at Cardoness for the whole war because obviously there was rationing then. I can remember this quite clearly. In the woods on either side of the lodge there were soldiers camping and Mother was friendly with some of them. I remember one who came, and he wrote poetry which was something I loved. There was a spare room in the lodge and he would sit there writing. There was another soldier who was very kind and he would occasionally come on picnics. My mother was always packing them, and we would climb Mill Knock and have a picnic there. Of course we didn't hear a lot from my father because he was on the front line all that time.

The road went through to Stranraer where all the boats were, and the American convoys used to come through which was great for us children – we used to stand waiting and they used to throw us chewing gum and sweets - we were absolutely thrilled, we didn't know what such things were.

Everything was rationed in the war but we were kept fed by the estate, we never went hungry. But luxury things – I remember when I first saw a banana. Fruit was grown on the estate. Apart from the camps and the Americans I wasn't really aware of what was going on. I didn't worry about my father being killed although I missed him. After the war things were very different for everyone. It was much worse for the Rainsford-Hannays – the son Ramsay took it on and they've now got beautifully placed caravans dotted round the rocks. Ramsay's grandson and great grandchildren are still there. I went back 8 years ago to see a school friend who was dying of cancer. Everything was just the same – every rock, the little stream. The fishermen's nets were still there but were not being fished commercially. There was someone living in the Lodge.

The fishermen's nets

Skyreburn School

My school was a substantial granite building up the glen with a clear burn running alongside. There was one large classroom with lines of neat straight desks, a blackboard and a stove to keep us warm, with a mesh guard around it. Children from 5-11 were divided accordingly in this large room. The toilets were outside. There was a small room adjacent for extra teaching. There was drill every morning after the bell rang and we were lined up. Coats were hung up regimentally. My memories of spelling and sums are very clear. Tables were recited every morning endlessly and Mrs Marion Swan, the only teacher, the headmistress, would point at us with, 7 x 9 or 8 x 4 around the class, quickly. I remember the blackboard and the horrible screech of the chalk. Mrs Swan had two daughters herself.

Discipline was strict and behaviour was good, otherwise there was a rap across the knuckles with a ruler or worse. As for me, I got the black tawse across my palms for being late for lessons, mainly at lunch time when we walked home – about a mile - for a break and were distracted along the shore line on return. I walked barefoot along the shore. I can see her now – wallop, her leg lifted back with the effort behind the force of the black leather strap. I never learned.

Playtimes were fun, with skipping ropes twirling at each end with all-in-together rhymes; peevie stones (hopscotch) was popular, with chase and tag. One highlight for me was the wild flower collection up the glen, away from the school, along a narrow twisting road beside the clear, tinkling burn, with dry stone walls and sheep in the fields. Wild flowers were abundant and the idea was to collect as many varieties as possible in a posy which would be judged for a small prize. I remember ragged robin, red campion, to name a few. I was very pleased when I found two very exciting specimens on my nature walk one afternoon: the egg of a sand martin, which I found in a hole in a sand dune, and a flower which I found growing in the mud, the sea holly.

The school regime was not varied, but an excellent start to my education. Work had to be neat and words spaced out evenly. The 3 Rs were the most important with the arts rather far behind. The children on the estate attended the school, and the arrival of about 30 children who were evacuated from Glasgow at the outbreak of the Second World War swelled the numbers considerably. That was an exciting time for me. These poor kids had impetigo, which I caught on my hands. Violet gentian, a lurid purple ointment, was spread on the knuckles. Nits and head lice were also a problem. My mother spread a newspaper, and with a steel comb and paraffin, set to on my golden head of hair. The paraffin was delivered to my mother by a bloke from Gatehouse for her paraffin lamps and things. There was no electricity at all.

Passing Skyreburn school the little burn tumbled, sparkling in the sunlight over the boulders, and was a favourite place to catch a glimpse of a kingfisher and watch minnows in the clear water. With my mother we walked uphill to open moorland, a favourite place for autumn blackberry and rose hip picking.

I was nearly 12 when we left. I had just passed to go to Kirkudbright Academy from Gatehouse because after Skyreburn I went for not quite a year to Gatehouse School. That's where I passed the exam and would have gone to Kirkcudbright Academy, but then it was moving time for my parents so I ended up at Lockerbie Academy for a short time.

The People

The Gordon Family

The big lodge on the first entrance to the sweeping drive of Cardoness House was lived in by the Gordon family after Laurie Jennings left for Canada with his parents. I loved visiting and playing with Ethel and Margaret. Ethel, the younger sister, was rather a dim girl, always scratching her head and grinning, perhaps because we all had nits in our hair during that time. Margaret, my age, around 8 years, was very pretty and for me, at last, a girl to walk to Skyreburne school with and to join in on adventurous shore walks. The household, in great contrast to my own, was a pickle, but tremendous fun as we were allowed a free rein. Mr Gordon was much older than his wife, and to me a very old man. He had a constant dew drip on the end of his nose which would fall into the can of milk which he noisily drank from. Pulled toffee, made by Mrs Gordon, was a favourite, and literally we could pull it into long strips before chewing. Beech nuts were sometimes added to this delicious toffee.

Dooking for apples at Halloween and catching a bite from an apple attached to a long string added to the fun in the Big Lodge living room. We were allowed to slide downstairs on a none-too-clean bare mattress. Mr Gordon always sat in an old chair. I am not certain what else he ever did. Mrs Gordon worked as a cleaner at Cardoness House. They were there because Mrs Gordon was very useful in the house.

Angus Gillespie, the shepherd

Mr Gillespie, shepherd to Sir William Maxwell and Colonel Rainsford-Hannay for 50 years, lived alone with his dog in a remote cottage in the Galloway hills.

Angus Gillespie's sheep and butt and ben (where he lived) in the background

With his crook and faithful dog, he knew where all the sheep were on the moors, and sometimes walked over the hills to Cardoness where the housekeeper would bottle feed some of the lambs in the kitchen. Mother never thought it necessary to go away during the long school holidays as all we needed was on our doorstep. An annual treat which always stays in my memory, and was usually done about two weeks before the school term began, was the bus ride to

Angus Gillespie and friend on Dromore

his remote shepherd's cottage at Dromore. Laurie came with us and we climbed slowly, higher and higher away from the seashore and into the heather clad slopes beyond Gatehouse.

This weekly bus made the trip to the railway station on Dromore to collect large parcels and to deposit the few passengers who were lucky enough to have a relative up there in the wilds. Sheep grazed by the roadside, which was a rough track for the last part of our journey. We would see the viaduct on a clear day. My mother had packed a picnic with fresh scones and a fruitcake for Angus. His stone dwelling seemed to appear out of the heather out of the vast craggy hillside where peregrine falcons were seen.

The train going through the Clints of Dromore

To get to the cottage, we always had to take our shoes off and paddle across a clear tinkling burn, being careful not to slip on the curiously white smooth boulders, all adding to the fun.

The nearest neighbour to Angus was a small station master's cottage. After our picnic mother brought the latest news from Cardoness as we played near the grazing sheep, listening to the plaintive cry of the curlew and the whirring of the startled grouse in flight from its cover. Our calls to each other echoed and re-echoed under the arches of the old viaduct. We played safely and happily until the sun began to dip and it was time to join Angus and mother. We were hungry and well ready for the supper they had prepared for us, and the welcoming bark of Ken, the collie dog.

Angus told us he had more than enough of all the good things in life. Many years later I understood what he meant.

Angus Farmer, the dry stane dyker (dry stone waller)

Angus Farmer was the full time dry stane dyker for the estate and employed by Colonel Rainsford-Hannay. He and his wife had two daughters and they lived in a pretty cottage down Skyreburn Lane. The Colonel was an authority on this ancient craft and every now and again Angus would get his orders from him. New walls and repairs were ongoing and the stones were from the granite quarry near Creetown. The estate was extensive and every day Angus, in a thick coat and trousers tied with string would cycle to work with his piece (lunch), a bottle of cold tea and onion and cheese between thick slices of bread. Every Saturday night Angus would bike to the Angel in Gatehouse for a pint or two, then push the bike back the three miles to his cottage.

The Angel hotel in the High Street, Gatehouse of Fleet

Photo courtesy Brian McMurray

Competitions were on every year and a cup presented to the best craftsman. A proud Angus won on one occasion.

As with all the estate workers the free cottage was provided, plus two loads of coal and wood from the estate. The wage was 35/- a week. They had two children, Cecil and Betty. Betty was frail, with a chest complaint. They were real proud Scottish folk and cod liver oil and clothes, and nappies, provided by the Rainsford-Hannays, were delivered to them via my mother.

As was the custom there was a good back garden where all the vegetables were grown and a few scraggy hens which never seemed to lay any eggs. I was always made welcome and I well remember raiding the larder and eating handfuls of raisins which had become rather stale. Although there was porridge for breakfast, I don't think Mrs Farmer enjoyed cooking.

Gardener's Cottage – the gardener before Mr Broadfoot

Photo courtesy Brian McMurray

Charlie Broadfoot, the head gardener

He lived with his wife in a substantial stone house just yards from the walled garden where he was employed as head gardener. He was assisted by Geordie and Belle McDermot. The garden was sectioned off by long grass paths leading to the shore and the secluded bathing hut. The walks were lined with rhododendrons, a beautiful sight in the summer, with red, white and lilac blooms. The climate was ideal for growing apricots, peaches and, grapes as well as abundant soft fruit.

In the walled garden with my mother and her friend 1937

I remember helping Mrs Broadfoot string black currants ready for jam She was a motherly lady and I remember spitting prune stones into her hand and games in the big airy living room. I stayed with her for a few days when my sister Ann was born. I was 3 years and 8 months old. The extensive garden was surrounded by a high stone wall, enough to keep trespassers out.. There was usually a surplus of vegetables which was divided amongst the estate workers. An artichoke, dipped in fresh butter from the dairy, was a great treat. A memorable flavour.

Me with Mrs Broadfoot 1937

Jim Davidson, the fisherman

I will begin with Granny Davidson, the wife of Bob and mother of Jim, the fisherman. As the school day drew to a close, my thoughts strayed to the walk home. Granny Davidson, a bent, very old lady with a toothless grin, and wearing a black shawl, lived near the school, by the burn in a pretty lattice windowed fisherman's cottage, with a garden full of foxgloves. Her hot tattie scones, straight from the girdle, curled at the edges and dripping with butter were mine for the asking. For some years to follow before she died, there were tattie scones every evening until the last school girl had gone

Mr & Mrs Davidson, parents of Jim the fisherman

Jim, his wife and two sons, Sam and Bobby lived in an estate cottage less than 50 yards from the shore. The fishing rights belonged to Colonel Rainsford-Hannay.

Salmon fishing began in May and ended in October, a busy time as the nets were full. During the winter months Jim would clean and mend the nets which were spread out across the green behind his cottage. Stripped pieces of wood were used for the knitting. With the high spring tides the water spilled over the roads and into the low lying cottage garden.

My mother with Jim Davidson at the nets in Laundry Bay

I loved playing with Sam and Bobby and learnt to ride on an old sit-up-and-beg bike. I couldn't reach the saddle but pedalled furiously around the green, falling off frequently, but luckily with no harm done. In the low white washed cottage Mrs Davidson was busy baking. A girdle hung from a hook over the open fire. Wood and coal provided by the Rainsford-Hannays was the main source for all cooking – delicious tattie scones, three cornered treacle scones, drop scones and oat cakes stood on end to dry and were then placed in a wooden box lined with a tea towel. During the height of the season visitors would stay at Cardoness House and Jim, a striking character, in his waders, navy pullover, flat cap would deliver fresh trout and salmon to the kitchen in readiness for dinner. Any surplus was shared among the workers, and I remember flounders tied on a string and still wriggling were brought to the Old Lodge for mother to cook for tea.

Willie McMath, the head groom

Willie was employed as a groom at Cardoness House and lived in a nice house at the side of the stable yard. Before the outbreak of the Second World War, Mrs Rainsford-Hannay used to ride sidesaddle for miles across the sand at low tide. There was a granite mounting stone in the yard. The four horses were immaculately groomed and always ready for Mrs Rainsford-Hannay and her guests. Eventually cars took their place, and Willie had to don the chauffeur's uniform to take her ladyship out. He stayed there during the war as he was too old for call up.

Carriage and horses in the stable yard at Cardoness House

Photo courtesy Brian McMurray

Mrs McMath used to take the Sunday school, held in her front room and I remember walking with Ann from the Old

Lodge along the beech wood path, covered in primroses in April. After the war the stables were converted into offices and a hall for little social events.

Willie McMath's son, a keen mechanic, died from an infected boil at 17 years of age. There were no antibiotics and only the hardiest survived.

Bob McCormick, the gamekeeper

Bob McCormick was the only keeper for the estate and a familiar figure in tweed plus fours, a tweed jacket, a hat with a pheasant's feather in it. With his spaniel, gun and ferret in a box his day began. Rabbit burrows were all around the estate and ferrets were carried in a little wooden box with a lid on. It was lifted out by the scruff of the neck because of biting and placed at the entrance to a rabbit hole to chase the rabbit out at the other end and into the net. The rabbits were killed and gutted on sight, then placed in pairs on a pole, then carried over the gamekeeper's shoulder to the big house kitchen to be prepared for the dining table. Any surplus rabbits were for the estate workers and my mother would skin and prepare them for a delicious rabbit stew.

Bob with his coops

Pheasant shooting took place in the autumn, a very busy time for Bob. Parties of friends of the Rainsford-Hannay's went on drives to where the beaters flushed out the birds. Bob would load for the guests and the shoot began, the spaniel retrieving the birds, dropping them at the gamekeeper's feet.

There was a game larder in the woods where the birds had to hang for a certain time before eating. Only at Christmas did the workers get a free bird. My mother, a gamekeeper's daughter, was a dab hand at pheasant plucking. Bob and his wife eventually retired from the house in Laundry bay to a little cottage at Mossyard on the estate.

The McCormicks outside their retirement cottage

The Rainsford-Hannays would give the workers a house for their retirement, not a pension. They made sure they were all right, and gave them odd jobs. It was quite difficult for the rich as well after the war. The way of life for them, the change, the austerity was hard for them.

Dr Craig

Dr Craig was a tall and dignified gentleman who lived in Gatehouse-of-Fleet, and, when needed, he would call on the sick for a small sum of money. There was no National Health Service during my childhood. I remember when we were not very well, being dosed with syrup of figs and sulphur and treacle – something to do with the digestive system. For minor injuries, my mother would take me on the bus to his surgery, an imposing granite house reached by four very steep steps, and a brass doorbell to ring. When my sister had conjunctivitis (pinkeye) Dr Craig advised my mother to get rid of a white cat which apparently had caused the infection. Whooping cough "ran its course" with time off school; a Vick rub was applied to chests, and various ointments such as vaseline for cuts and scraped knees, and warm olive oil for earache. Threadworms, which I picked up from eating "soury clocks" – sorrel leaves - were soon cured by some potent mixture of my mother's. I will never forget the chloroform bag over my face – the sweet smell, and a faraway drifting off to sleep sensation when my adenoids were removed. I am sure my mother saved her pennies for medical attention, and gave what she could afford. Dr Craig no doubt made a decent living from visits to the local gentry, and the more affluent folk in Gatehouse.

Gatehouse of Fleet

This was our nearest shopping town and a trip on the two hourly bus from Stranraer to Dumfries was always looked forward to. Shoes were bought at Miss Trainer's in the High Street. My mother made sure that our feet were measured twice yearly with Clarks lace ups for winter and strap button shoes for best, and sandals for summer. Miss Trainer, a spinster lady, lived with her bachelor brother above the shop. I remember her in a brown overall climbing the step ladder to reach all those boxes on the top shelf.

Looking towards the High Street, Gatehouse of Fleet

Photo courtesy Brian McMurray

There was McAdams' shop, a general grocery store and delivery service. When in town we always had a bag of dolly mixtures at the counter. Every week the delivery van drew up at the Lodge gates and at Christmas time Mr McAdam gave his customers a small gift.

Willy Wilson, a jolly character, had a fish and fruit shop in the High Street and delivered twice weekly, kippers and smoked haddock. Willy would take a wireless battery away and recharge it for mother, bringing it back the following week, and would never charge a penny. Stark the chemist, situated by the clock tower and one of the two bus stops in Gatehouse, was very convenient. Bus drivers would return and collect prescriptions to be dropped off at the Lodge gates for the big house.

From Skyreburn School I was transferred to Gatehouse School to sit for the exam for Kirkcudbright Academy. In the control class my knowledge was widened and new friends were made. My best friend was Margaret Cameron – red headed, fiery tempered and great fun. I often stayed at her house and was fascinated by her father who was a watch and clockmaker. Her parents owned their own house. Margaret and I roamed the shore together and I remember clearly hiding in the Rainsford-Hannays' bathing hut and having a first puff on a cigarette supplied by Margaret's older brother. Cycling was allowed between Cardoness and Gatehouse and we had both passed our proficiency tests. I was now the proud owner of a new black Raleigh drop handlebar bicycle, bought by my father with his demob money. In that final school year, Margaret won the coveted Sports Club Cup and I passed the exam for Kirkcudbright Academy.

My school friend Jessie Margaret Cameron aged 11 years with the coveted school Sports Cup 1945

Me with the bike my father bought me with his demob money 1945

The Crosbie sisters, Audrey and Anne were my friends when I attended Gatehouse school. Their father Bob Crosbie owned the local garage at the top end of High Street, Gatehouse-of-Fleet. They lived in an imposing granite house with steep stone steps and iron railings, almost opposite the Angel Hotel. I remember playing in their large sitting room, while my mother and Mrs Crosbie caught up with the local gossip over tea and fruit cake. Audrey, who was my age, was always invited to birthday parties at the Old Lodge. She lives today in Catherine Street, Gatehouse-of-Fleet.

Epilogue

After the Second World War ended, life was very different and difficult for everyone, and it was time to "pick up the pieces" and move on as there was no longer a butler required at Cardoness House. Over the next five years my parents lived in five different tied cottages, my father working as a gardener cum handyman or chauffeur at big houses across England. My mother did her share by cleaning, or minding the young children. I attended Lockerbie Academy, Witney Grammar School, and finally Holton Park Girls Grammar School.

I survived a serious car accident at the age of twelve, consequently falling behind with my school work. These were hard but character forming years, and at aged sixteen years I finally persuaded my parents to gain independence and have a home of their own. This was a three bedroomed terrace house in Maidcroft Road, Cowley, Oxford where my mother lived for the next 50 years until her death aged 93 years. As a nurse and carer she was well known and liked in the area. My father until retirement was a security guard at the car factory.

Leaving school, my life unfolded. After a summer in Germany, I began my career in Library Services at 17 years old. Nine years later, in 1960, I married Martin, my German husband. We settled in Garsington in a 17th century thatched cottage, where I have lived for 56 years. During this time I had two children and sadly lost my sister Ann to cancer at 45 years of age. Now widowed, aged 81 years I enjoy a peaceful life, with my cat and tortoise, and many friends and interests, and most of all every aspect of the beautiful surrounding countryside in Oxfordshire. My idyllic childhood has helped make me the person I am today. Without these memories this book would not have been possible.

This part of Galloway has changed very little, and I have spent holidays there with my family, and on my own, reliving a memorable part of my life. I am well blessed. The jigsaw is complete.

Marion Gunther
Garsington 2016

Publications

Poetry:

Past and Present. 1972 Outpost Pub

The Old Museum Poets. 1997

Local History - Oxfordshire Books

Walking. An Appreciation of Garsington. 1990. OCC Pub

Garsington in Old Photographs. 1993. Alan Sutton Pub
Second edition. 2007. Pocket Images Nonsuch Pub Ltd

Around Wheatley in Old Photographs. 1995. Alan Sutton Pub

ND - #0274 - 080726 - C0 - 229/152/5 - PB - 9781784562915 - Gloss Lamination